I do not wish to gosip but...
and I am not saying it is not all
PERFECTLY inosent, but ... the cat, Horse,
has this (AHEM) frend... who can only
be described as unconvenchunal
unconveis. uncashus ~~farst, loos and weerd~~ not the sort of female I wood
wont a little boy of <u>mine</u> hangin out
WITH, thank you very much
my deer !!!
    I am sure she is very.... nice...
but can wun hav a cup of tea and
a chockylate oat bran biscuit with
a ... person... wot has a THING about
lether ?!!!?? <u>AND</u> tattooed ears !!!!??
Still, I no it takes all sorts— and fAr
be it from me to ~~critisise~~ ~~crickitsize~~
slag her off... so here is all wot
I cood find out about the she-cat called fred. ('fred', indeed! is this a name or wot you call a egg wot has fallen in a hot pan of fat ?!!)

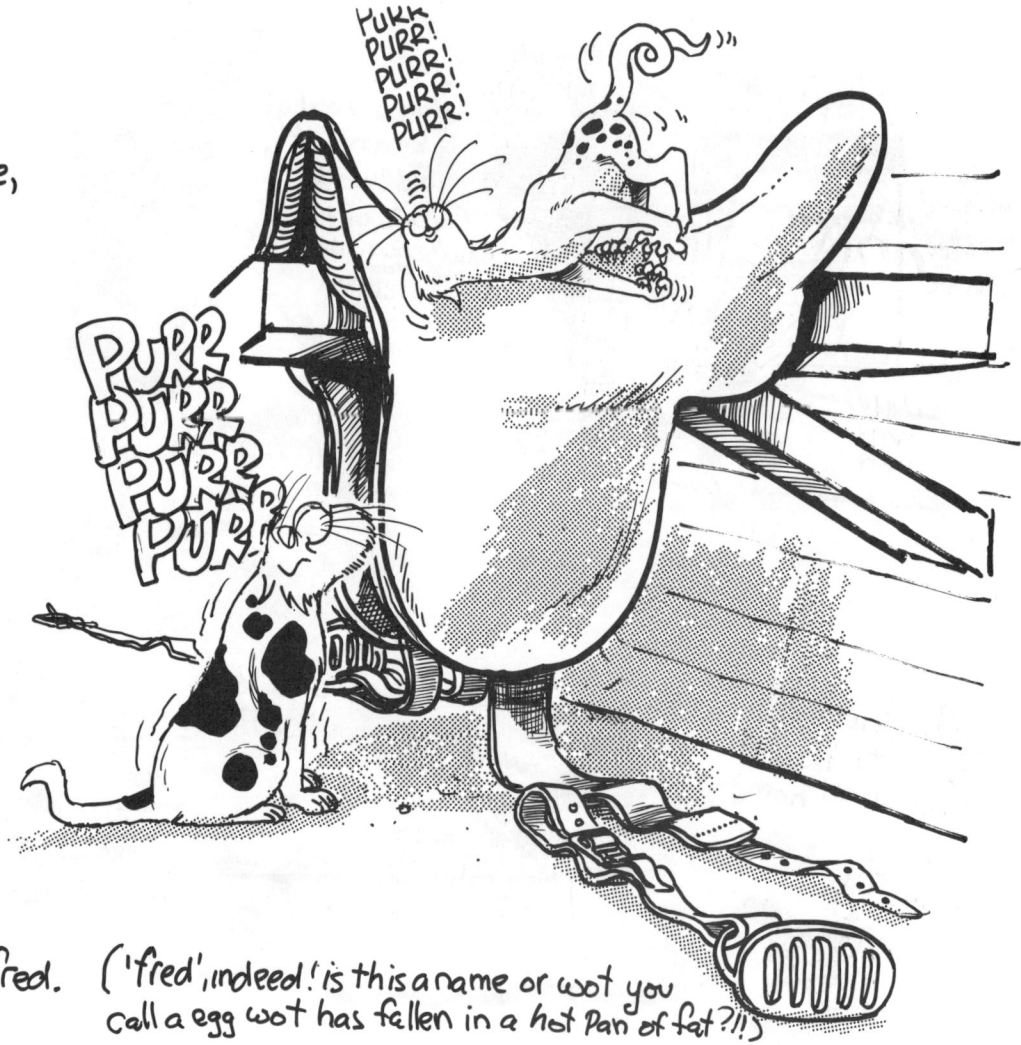

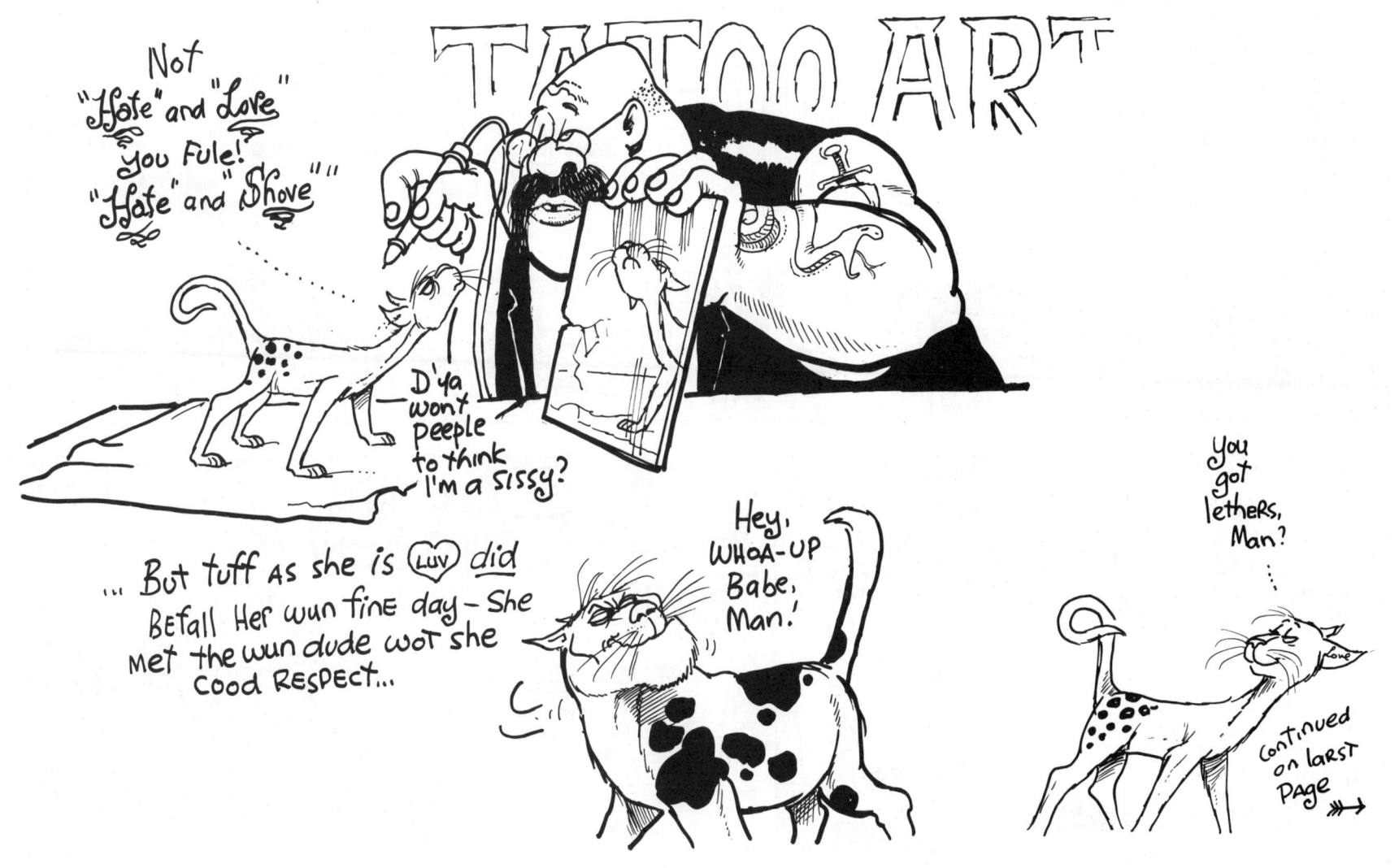

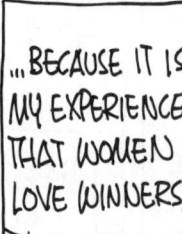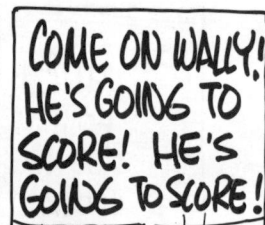

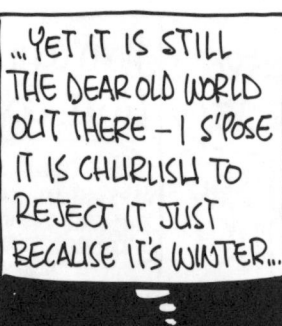

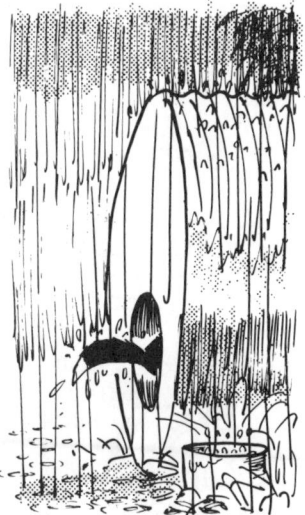

Page twenty

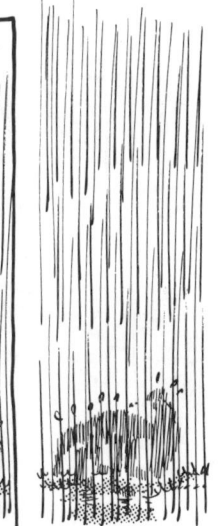

WELL, I WAS SORRY FOR RANGI JONES BEIN' IN THE FASHION SHOW...
© 1991 Diogenes Designs Ltd
...BUT NOW I KNOW HE ONLY DID IT TO BE WITH PASSION HUNGERFORD I CAN ENJOY IT WHEN THE AUDIENCE GIVES HIM HEAPS!
...AND HERE IS RANGI LAID BACK FOR SUMMER IN BRIEF, STRETCH SWIMMING TRUNKS..
WAIT FOR IT...
YAY! PHEEP! PHEEP! WOW! COOL! PHEE... EEEP!! CLAP.. APPLAUD! WHISTLE! STAMP! STAMP!
FF4187
OH YES, VERY SOPHISTICATED

MAN, DID YOU MAKE A FOOL OF YOURSELF TONIGHT RANGI JONES!?
HALL BACK STAGE
© 1991 Diogenes Designs Ltd
A BLOKE IN A FASHION SHOW! ARE YOU GONNA GET HEAPS FROM YOUR MATES AT SCHOOL TOMORROW!
FF4188
I SAID, "YOU'RE GONNA BE TORN APART BY THE KIDS AT SCHOOL TOMORROW!"
OKAY, DON'T SAY I DIDN'T WARN YOU!!

Page thirty eight

Page thirty nine

Page forty

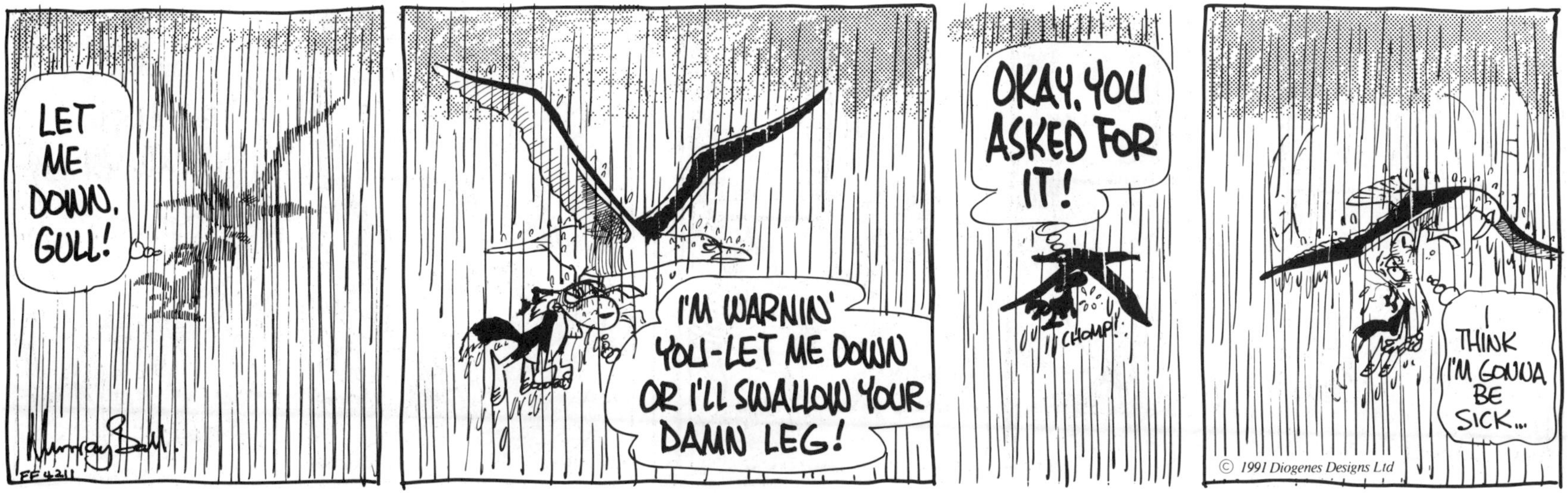
LET ME DOWN, GULL!
I'M WARNIN' YOU-LET ME DOWN OR I'LL SWALLOW YOUR DAMN LEG!
OKAY, YOU ASKED FOR IT!
CHOMP!
I THINK I'M GONNA BE SICK...
Murray Ball.
FF 4211
© 1991 Diogenes Designs Ltd

I THINK MY RUTHLESSNESS IN SWALLOWING THE GULL'S LEG IS PAYIN' OFF — WE ARE COMING DOWN...
HOLD ON, THAT IS WATER BELOW!
YOU ROTTEN SEAGULL! YOU ARE BRINGIN' ME DOWN IN THE OCEAN!!
SPLOSH!
GET UP AND HELP WITH THE LAMBIN' YA USELESS MONGREL!
I CAN'T- MY MOUTH TASTES OF BAD FISH AND ATHLETES FOOT...
Murray Ball.
FF 4212
© 1991 Diogenes Designs Ltd

Page forty two

Page forty three

GRRRRRRR
POK! POK! POK! POK! POK! POK! POK!
ARE YOU MAD? I'M A DOG !!!
1991 Diogenes Designs Ltd
FF 4245

I'VE JUST BEEN ASSAULTED BY A ROOSTER IN MY OWN HOME!
I CAN'T BELIEVE THIS! BIRDS DON'T ATTACK DOGS!
OI! WHAT'S WITH YOU DICKY BIRD?!
POK! POK! POK! POK! POK! POK! POK! POK!
OKAY, RICHARD BIRD
1991 Diogenes Designs Ltd
FF 4246

Page forty five

WAL'!!
© 1991 Diogenes Designs Ltd
FF4249
YE GODS, HE'S COMIN'! HE'LL FIND HIS TOUGH, MACHO DOG BOTTLED UP IN THE HEN RUN BY A TRUCULENT ROOSTER – WHAT A DISGRACE!
JUST PUTTIN' IN A BIT OF WORK ON THE OLD UNEVEN BARS, WAL'...
Murray Ball.

FF4251
HEY UNCLE WAL', THE DOG IS SCARED OF THE ROOSTER!
"SCARED OF THE ROOSTER"?!! I'LL SHOW YOU WHO'S SCARED OF THE ROOSTER...
SMAK!
© 1991 Diogenes Designs Ltd
THAT'S WHO'S SCARED OF THE ROOSTER!
Murray Ball.

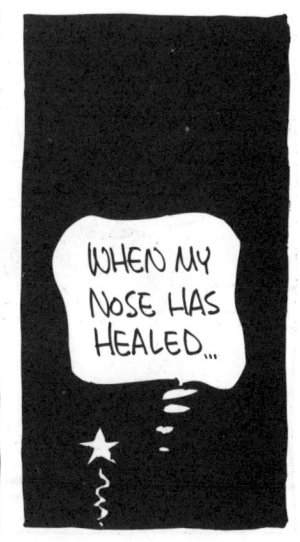

Page forty seven

... AND D'Y KNOW WHAT I LIKE MOST ABOUT THE "EASY CARE" METHOD OF LAMBIN' COOCHIE?
... IT'S NOT HAVIN' THOSE PAIN-IN-THE-NECK, BOTTLE-FED PET LAMBS TRAILIN' UNDER MY FEET....
JOG! JOG! JOG! JOG!
DON'T LOOK UPON HER AS A PET, DEAR, SO MUCH AS A TINY LIFE YOUR KINDNESS HAS SAVED FROM AN UNTIMELY END...
SUCK SUCK SUCK
1991 Diogenes Designs Ltd
FF 4237
Murray Ball.

AW HELL'S BELLS, AUNTY!!
ZONK! ZONK! ZONK! ZONK
I'VE ACCEPTED YOU'VE GOT A PET LAMB, BUT DO YOU HAVE TO KEEP LITTLE DOTTY IN THE HOUSE?!!
ZONK! ZONK! ZONK! ZONK! ZONK!
FF 4238
OH, THAT IS NOT DOTTY, DEAR
© 1991 Diogenes Designs Ltd
... THIS IS DOTTY...
... I'M AFRAID THAT IS GEORGE.
Murray Ball.

YOU'VE GOT WHAT?!!
© 1991 Diogenes Designs Ltd
...YOU'VE GOT FOURTEEN ORPHANNED LAMBS IN YOUR BEDROOM?
FF 4239
WHO'S GONNA LOOK AFTER THEM WHEN YOU GO BACK TO TAURANGA?!!
OH? D'Y RECKON IT'S WORTH A TRY?
OH ♫ COOCHIE...
Murray Ball.

I'VE GOT FOURTEEN FLAMIN' ORPHANED LAMBS AND COOCH IS NOT HOME!
WHO'S GONNA LOOK AFTER THEM?? WHO'S GONNA LOOK AFTER THEM??
Murray Ball.
PERHAPS I CAN NARROW IT DOWN A BIT...
FF 4240
NOT ME!! NOT ME!!
© 1991 Diogenes Designs Ltd

Page fifty

OKAY MRS JONES, YOU WIN. I'D LIKE TO SWOP THE BOX OF PUPPIES YOU GAVE ME FOR THE LAMBS I GAVE PUTI...
SNATCH!
ARE YOU MAD? PEBBLES FOR PEARLS?!!
© 1991 Diogenes Designs Ltd
FF 4243
Murray Ball.

THIS IS RIDICULOUS— EXPLAINING MYSELF TO A DOG...
LOOK, DOG, FOR THE LAST TIME - I DID NOT SWAP THE PUPPIES FOR THE LAMBS BECAUSE I PREFER SHEEP TO DOGS...
FF 4244
...IT'S JUST THAT SHEEP ARE EASIER TO MANAGE AND DISPOSE OF THAN DOGS.
I SEE, YES THAT IS TRUE...
...AS A MATTER OF FACT THEY ARE HARDLY EVEN HUMAN, ARE THEY?
© 1991 Diogenes Designs Ltd
Murray Ball.

I HAVEN'T BEEN TO THE BACK OF THE FARM SINCE THE STORM
GOOD GRACIOUS, THIS SLIP MUST HAVE CAUGHT ALL THOSE SHEEP AND CRUSHED OR BURIED THEM!
WHAT A TRAGIC WASTE OF LIFE!
...AND FOOD!!
© 1991 Diogenes Designs Ltd

WHAT A MESS! DEMOLISHED FENCES COLLAPSED HILLSIDES DEAD STOCK...
THE STORM HAS CREATED A SCENE OF UGLINESS AND DESOLATION
STILL, ON THE BRIGHT SIDE...
MAGNIFICENT AROMA!
© 1991 Diogenes Designs Ltd

WHAT A TRAGEDY. ALL THOSE SHEEP KILLED IN A MUD SLIDE
© 1991 Diogenes Designs Ltd
...YET ALL I CAN THINK ABOUT IS, DO I STAY AND EAT THEM LIKE MY PRIMITIVE ANCESTORS OR DO I GO HOME TO TEA AS I HAVE BEEN TAUGHT?
FF 4232
Murray Ball
I'M IN ORBIT

DO I EAT THE DEAD SHEEP IN THE SLIP OR GO HOME LIKE A GOOD DOG?
© 1991 Diogenes Designs Ltd
FF 4233
PERHAPS I AM NOT TOO LATE... PERHAPS I COULD SAVE ONE...
OH DEAR... A BIT HAS COME OFF— WHAT SHALL I DO WITH IT?
DROP THAT YA SCUNGY MONGREL!!
WHAK!
THANK GOD! AT LAST, A DECISION!
Murray Ball.

Page fifty four

WHIFFLE... WHUFF!
© 1991 Diogenes Designs Ltd
FF 4227
SNUFFLE WHIMPH GRIMPH GRRMMPH!
HOWL...OOOOWWWWLLLLL
WHAT D'Y DO WHEN THE SEXIEST SHE-WOLF IN THE PACK IS IN SEASON AND YOU ARE NUMBER FORTY-FOUR IN THE PECKING ORDER?
Murray Ball

LOOK AT THE DOG, HE'S DREAMING
SNUFFLE! WHIFFLE! SNIF! SNUK!
FF 4228
HEH HEH! PROBABLY DREAMING OF WOOLLY, WHITE SHEEP—CHASING THEM OVER WIDE, GREEN, SUN-DAPPLED HILLS
WUFFLE! WOOF! WIFF! WUFF! SNUKKLE!
© 1991 Diogenes Designs Ltd
ZZZ SNUFFLE ZZZ
...AS WE ARE LOCKED IN THIS WARM, DARK CAVE ALL NIGHT, SHE-WOLF GREEN EYES, I THOUGHT YOU AND I MIGHT... CHUCKLE SNUFFLE
CUTE DOG.
Murray Ball

NUMBER 44, GRYMPH! WHY SHOULDN'T I BE NUMBER ONE IN THE WOLF PACK? WHY SHOULDN'T IT BE ME WITH THAT SEXY SHE-WOLF? GRYMPH! GRUMBLE! MUMBLE!
NNNN
© 1991 Diogenes Designs Ltd
Murray Ball
FF 4229
CLANG!!
"GETTING UPPITY"? ME? OH GOSH NO MR. SAW JAW, SIR. I WAS JUST WANTING TO WISH YOU AND SHE-WOLF GREEN EYES A HAPPY AND SUCCESSFUL UNION, SIR. (SIGH!)

HULLO, THERE ARE A COUPLE OF GOATS CAUGHT IN THAT HUGE BLACKBERRY BUSH – I'D BETTER CALL WAL'
FF 4220
WOOF! WOOF! WOOF! WOOF! WOOF! WOOF! WOOF!
WOOF! WOOF! WOOF! WOOF! WOOF!
WOOF! WOOF! WOOF! WOOF! WOOF! WOOF! WOOF!
© 1991 Diogenes Designs Ltd
CLONK!
Murray Ball
OH, YOU KNOW

Page fifty seven

Page fifty eight

IT'S OKAY DOG, I'VE STRUCK THE BOTTOM OF THE DITCH...
NOBLE WAL' HAS PLUNGED INTO THE BLACKBERRY TO RESCUE TWO STUCK GOATS
Murray Ball
... I'M JUST GOIN' TO CRAWL ALONG THE DRAIN UNTIL IT COMES OUT OF THE BUSH...
BRAVE LAD!
FF 4225
© 1991 Diogenes Designs Ltd
I CAN SEE LIGHT!
THANK HEAVENS YOU'RE SAFE!

BRAVE, BATTERED WAL' HAS RESCUED THE GOATS FROM THE BLACKBERRY BUSH!
STAND BACK DOG, I'M CHUCKIN' 'EM UP ONTO THE TOP!
© 1991 Diogenes Designs Ltd
FF4226
NOW, ALL I'VE GOT TO DO IS GET MYSELF UP...
HEAVE! STRAIN! SCRAMBLE!
PHEW! RIGHTO, WHERE DID THEY GO?
Murray Ball.

Page sixty

I CAN'T UNDERSTAND WHY THAT POOFY CORGI IS SO POPULAR...
Murray Ball.
RUB! RUB! RUB!
FF4260
SLAM!
WHAT MORE CAN I DO?
© 1991 Diogenes Designs Ltd

PAT! PAT! STROKE
FF4261
SHOVE!
© 1991 Diogenes Designs Ltd
ARE YOU MAD?!

Page sixty two

Page sixty three

LOOK, A DOG HANGIN' IN A TREE
© 1991 Diogenes Designs Ltd
IT LOOKS AS IF SOME LEOPARD OR GREAT CAT HAS HUNG HIM THERE TO DEVOUR AT ITS LEISURE.
FF4315
D'Y RECKON WE SHOULD GET HIM DOWN?
I THINK THAT WOULD BE MOST UNWISE FOR WE OURSELVES MIGHT BECOME TARGETS FOR THIS KILLER CAT!
YOU COULD AT LEAST TURN ME UP THE OTHER WAY - ALL THE BLOOD IS RUNNING TO MY TOES!!
Murray Ball

AH, HORSE. YOU'VE COME BACK...
Murray Ball
© 1991 Diogenes Designs Ltd
...LOOK, I'VE BEEN THINKING OVER OUR LITTLE DISPUTE AND I FEEL I HAVE BEEN A LITTLE TOO UNCOOPERATIVE...
FF4316
...I'VE DECIDED TO SHARE MY LITTLE SECRET WITH YOU - THERE ARE TEN BABY RABBITS IN THAT BURROW...
SHOVE!
DEAR HORSE, MAGNANIMOUS AS EVER

I CRACKED UNDER TORTURE AND TOLD HORSE ABOUT THE YOUNG RABBITS IN THE BURROW...
I'VE GOT TO WARN THEM!
© 1991 Diogenes Designs Ltd
FF4317
OH NO! TEN LITTLE PAIRS OF EARS! HE MUST HAVE FOUND THE RABBITS BY HIMSELF!
THANK HEAVENS...
...I'M NOT GUILTY!
Murray Ball

LOOK WAL', IT'S THEM, THE GOATS WHO'VE BEEN EATING YOUR TREES!
Murray Ball
WHAT A COINCIDENCE – US OUT RABBIT SHOOTIN' AND FINDIN' THOSE ROGUE GOATS,
AT LAST, EH WAL'? WE'VE GOT THEM!
FF4262
WELL COME ON... WHAT ARE YOU WAITING FOR?
NO I DIDN'T KNOW THE MOST FEARED ANIMAL IN THE JUNGLE WAS A WOUNDED BILLY GOAT!
© 1991 Diogenes Designs Ltd

WAL' IS HAVIN' A POT AT ONE OF THE TREE-EATING FERAL GOATS...
KRAK!
Y' GOT HIM BUT Y' DIDN'T BOWL HIM!
C'MON. Y' CAN'T LEAVE A WOUNDED ANIMAL!
WAL'?
SOB!
PULL YOURSELF TOGETHER MAN!
SLAP! SLAP! SLAP!
© 1991 Diogenes Designs Ltd
FF 4263
Murray Ball

I THINK THE WOUNDED GOAT IS HIDING IN THIS PATCH OF SCRUB...
CRACK!
A MOVEMENT! OVER THERE WAL' - WE'RE ON TO HIM!
WAL'?
C'MON WAL' IT'S A WOUNDED GOAT NOT A WOUNDED BUFFALO!
© 1991 Diogenes Designs Ltd
FF 4264
Murray Ball

Page sixty seven

I GOT ONE OF THE BLASTED PINE-EATING FERAL GOATS, EH DOG?
FF4267
... S'POSE A MAN SHOULD TAKE A TROPHY AFTER A SUCCESSFUL HUNT, EH?
I BELIEVE THE EAR IS TRADITIONAL...
GOOD IDEA WAL' - WHICH EAR D'Y WANT...
... THE CLEAN ONE OR THE ONE WITH THE PRETTY YELLOW TAG?
© 1991 Diogenes Designs Ltd
Murray Ball

I HEARD A SHOT FROM FOOTROT'S PLACE!
HEY FOOTROT! HAVE YOU SEEN A YELLOW-TAGGED BILLY?
IT'S A MURPHY GOAT!
© 1991 Diogenes Designs Ltd
FF4268
CUHUMP!
AREN'T YOU GOING TO BE JUST A WEE BIT ASHAMED OF YOURSELF IN THE MORNING WAL'?
Murray Ball

Page sixty nine

WHUMP!
AW HELL, KITTENS!
RATBAGS WHO SHIRK THEIR RESPONSIBILITIES SHOULD BE SHOT!
BANG!
Murray Ball
FF 4291
© 1991 Diogenes Designs Ltd

WAL' IS REALLY MAD AT THE PEOPLE WHO DUMPED A SACK OF KITTENS ON US
GRRROOM!!!
Murray Ball
FF 4292
WE'RE GOIN' TO RETURN THEM
WHAK! WHAK! WHAK!
THIS SACK BELONG TO YOU?
YEH
© 1991 Diogenes Designs Ltd
SHAKE! SHAKE!
TA

S'POSE I'D BETTER GIVE THE POOR LITTE SODS SOME JELLYMEAT...
WAL' DIDN'T MANAGE TO GIVE BACK THE DUMPED KITTENS...
FF4293
SWIPE!
SLAM!!
WHAT DO YOU CARE IF JELLYMEAT TURNS SOME FATHERLESS KITTENS INTO WHIMPS, HORSE?
GNAW! GNAW! RIP! BITE
TEAR! CHOMP!
© 1991 Diogenes Designs Ltd
Murray Ball.

I MEAN THE CHEEK OF THESE GUYS, COOCH, DUMPIN' A SACK OF KITTENS AT MY PLACE!
© 1991 Diogenes Designs Ltd
FF4294
I MEAN, WHY MY PLACE? WHAT'S IT GOT TO DO WITH ME?!!
OI, JUST ONE MOMENT, HORSE...!
Murray Ball

Page seventy two

THE KITTENS DON'T SEEM TO LIKE ANYTHING HORSE GIVES THEM TO EAT...
MEEOW! MEEOW! MEEOW MEEOW
I THINK HE IS WORRIED
FF 4297
HE'S FINDING MOTHERS HAVE SKILLS EVEN HE DOES NOT POSSESS
HOWEVER HE IS LEARNING TO ADAPT...
© 1991 Diogenes Designs Ltd
Murray Ball

I MUST SAY HORSE IS DOIN' HIS BEST AS A SOLO PARENT
Murray Ball.
FF 4298
HE'S TEACHIN' THE KITTENS TO HUNT ...
... AND FEND FOR THEMSELVES
GRRRR...
OF COURSE, IT IS A GRADUAL PROCESS...
GRRRRRRR...
GRRR... GRRR... GRRR... GRRR... GRRR... GRRR
© 1991 Diogenes Designs Ltd

Page seventy four

PHEEEEP!!
C'MON MAJOR— WE'RE AFTER A PIG!
HMFF!
© 1991 Diogenes Designs Ltd
I NOTICE HE NEVER GETS ANY OF THE HARD JOBS - LIKE BRINGIN' IN THE SHEEP!!
FF4278
BRINGIN' IN SHEEP REQUIRES SKILL, A BIT OF FINESSE - DON'T BOTHER OLD BONE-BRAIN WITH ANYTHING LIKE THAT, WILL YOU!
ONLY THREE?
Murray Ball

IT MAKES ME SO MAD WHEN WAL' LEAVES ME BEHIND ON THE PIG HUNT AND TAKES THAT CANINE CAVEMAN, MAJOR.
Murray Ball
...I'D JUST LIKE TO SHOW HIM HOW A REAL DOG WOULD TANGLE WITH A HALF-TONNE TUSKER!
FF4279
...I'D LIKE TO SHOW HIM HOW A DOG OF CLASS FACES THE CHARGE. THE BULGING NECK MUSCLES, THE RAZOR TUSKS...
OH
STICK WITH THE BIG GUY. HE'S NOT HALF BAD!
© 1991 Diogenes Designs Ltd

I'M FREE
FATE HAS GRANTED MY WISH TO BE FREE TO SHOW WAL' JUST HOW GOOD I'D BE FACING A CHARGING TUSKER
ONE BLOODY FREE WISH AND I WISHED FOR THAT!!
© 1991 Diogenes Designs Ltd
FF4280
Murray Ball

I'VE BEEN GRANTED MY WISH – I AM FREE TO SHOW WAL' HOW GOOD I'D BE ON A PIG HUNT...
STILL, LOOKIN' ON THE BRIGHT SIDE...
... I MIGHT GET A NEAT, MACHO SCAR LIKE MAJOR HAS ON HIS SHOULDER
THAT IS THE BRIGHT SIDE?!!
© 1991 Diogenes Designs Ltd
FF4281
Murray Ball

HERE I AM IN THE BUSH LOOKIN' FOR AN OPPORTUNITY TO SHOW WAL' HOW GOOD I'D BE AT TACKLIN' A WILD PIG...
WHO AM I KIDDIN'? I'D BE A DISASTER! I'M A SHEEPDOG! A SHEEPDOG! A SHEEPDOG!
FF4282
I'M NOT A PIG-DOG'S REAR END!!
CRASH! SMASH!
IN FACT, YES I AM... I AM A PIG-DOG'S REAR END...
© 1991 Diogenes Designs Ltd

GET A HOLD OF YOURSELF DOG!
FF4283
SO YOU'VE BEEN CONFRONTED BY THE MIGHTY HERMIT RAM – SO YOU'RE A SHEEPDOG AREN'T YOU?!!
... IF THERE IS ONE THING YOU'RE GOOD AT IT IS CONTROLLING SHEEP – GET OUT THERE AND USE THE POWERS YOU WERE BORN WITH!
OKAY RAM, LET'S HAVE IT OUT – EYEBALL TO EYEBALL!
WELL YOU'RE JUST GONNA HAVE TO STAND ON YOUR BACK LEGS, AREN'T YOU?
© 1991 Diogenes Designs Ltd

Page seventy eight

Page seventy nine

PURR! PURR! PURR! PURR!
PURR! PURR! PURR! PURR! PURR! PURR! PURR! PURR! PURR
"Cool!"

Good gracious, I hope They are Married...
See you nekst year
Luv from The Dog - xxx